SOMETHING WONDERFUL HAPPENED

SOMETHING WONDERFUL HAPPENED

The First Easter for Beginning Readers

Matthew 28:1-10 FOR CHILDREN
Mark 16:1-11
Luke 24:1-12
John 20:1-18

by Joan Chase Bowden
illustrated by Aline Cunningham

I CAN READ A BIBLE STORY
Series Editor: Dorothy Van Woerkom

Publishing House
St. Louis

TO SANDY, ANDREW, AND
PAMELA JANE WITH LOVE

Concordia Publishing House, St. Louis, Missouri
Copyright © 1977 Concordia Publishing House

MANUFACTURED IN THE UNITED STATES OF AMERICA

Library of Congress Cataloging in Publication Data

Bowden, Joan Chase.
    Something wonderful happened.

    (I can read a Bible story)
    SUMMARY: Relates the events of the Resurrection.
    1. Jesus Christ—Resurrection—Juvenile litera-
ture. [1. Jesus Christ—Resurrection. 2. Easter]
I. Cunningham, Aline. II. Title.
BT481.B65   232.9'7   77-6325
ISBN 0-570-07324-3
ISBN 0-570-07318-9 pbk.

Something wonderful had happened!

But no one knew about it yet.

Jerusalem did not know it.

The city still slept

in the dark of Sunday morning.

The friends of Jesus

did not know it.

Sadly they walked along the path

to the garden

where Jesus was buried.

They carried jars of oils

and spices.

As they walked,

they talked about Jesus.

They talked about

how they had loved Him.

"But Jesus has died on the cross!"

cried Mary Magdalene.

"What will we do without Him?"

"This is the third day

since Jesus died," another woman said.

Her name was Mary, too.

"Now we must take these oils

and spices

to His tomb

and rub them on His body."

Then Joanna asked,

"But how will we roll away

the stone from the door

of the tomb?"

"It is very large," Salome said.

"It is too heavy for us to move."

For the rest of the way

they all wondered

who would move that heavy stone.

At last they came to the garden.

Low in the east

the sky grew pink.

The sun was slowly rising.

Tall grass
brushed against their cloaks.
Under their feet
wild flowers wet their sandals
with tiny drops of dew.

But the women did not see

the flowers

or the dew on their sandals.

They were looking at the tomb.

The stone was rolled back
from the door!

Quickly,

Mary Magdalene looked inside.

The tomb was empty!

"Someone has taken
our Lord away!" she cried.
"Who could have done
this awful thing?"

Mary Magdalene ran from the garden
to tell the news to Peter.
Peter was one
of the friends of Jesus.

But the other women
did not go with her.
"Can it be true?" they said.
"Has someone taken Jesus away?"
They went inside the tomb
to find out.

All at once

the tomb was filled with light.

The women saw two angels

dressed in bright, shining clothes.

The angels were sitting
on the flat stone
where Jesus had lain.
But Jesus was not there!
The women were frightened.

"Do not be afraid,"

the angels said.

"You are looking for Jesus,

who died on the cross.

But He is not here!

He has risen!

He is alive,

just as He told you He would be.

Don't you remember?"

Then they did remember.

Jesus had told them He would

come back to life!

"Go, now," said the angels.

"Go and tell all the friends

of Jesus.

Tell them the wonderful news."

The women hurried to Jerusalem.

They ran all the way.

But Mary Magdalene
was already in the city.
People crowded the narrow streets
in the morning sunlight.
They hurried to the marketplace
to buy the things they needed.

Some were talking with

their neighbors.

Some sat on the temple steps.

They called to Mary Magdalene

as she ran by.

But she did not stop for anyone.

She did not stop running
until she found Peter.

Peter was with John,

another friend of Jesus.

Their heads were bowed.

They were very sad, because

they thought Jesus was dead.

"Come quickly!" Mary Magdalene cried.

"Come with me to the tomb!

Someone has taken Jesus away,

and we do not know

where they have laid Him."

Peter and John
could not believe this.
They ran all the way
to the garden.

But John was a young man,
and Peter was old.

John ran faster than Peter.

He was the first
to reach the tomb.

John looked inside the tomb.

It was cool in there,

and very quiet.

"Look!" John cried

when Peter came.

Peter went into the tomb.

He saw the sheets

that had covered Jesus.

He saw the cloth

that had covered His head.

"What has happened?" Peter asked.

"Where is Jesus?"

The two men hurried home.

"What has happened?"

Peter said again.

They did not remember that
Jesus had told them He would
come back to life.

Mary Magdalene

came back to the garden.

She was crying

as she looked into the tomb.

And then she saw the angels.

"Woman, why do you cry?"
the angels asked.
"Because someone has taken
my Lord away," she said.
"I do not know where
they have laid Him."

Behind her in the garden,

someone spoke.

"Why are you crying?

Who are you looking for?"

Mary Magdalene turned around.

She saw a Stranger standing there.

She said, "Sir, did you take my Lord?

Tell me where He is,

and I will take Him away."

But the Stranger said,
"Mary!"

Now she knew who He was.

"Master!" she cried.

It was Jesus!

"Tell all My friends
that you have seen Me," Jesus said.
"Tell them that I am going
back to heaven."

Mary Magdalene smiled
with happiness.

Jesus was not dead
after all!

She ran out of the cool garden
and into the warm sunlight.

She soon came to the gates
of Jerusalem.

She could see the house
where all the friends of Jesus
were waiting.

"Something wonderful
has happened!" she cried
as she ran into the house.
"I have seen the Lord!"

And Mary Magdalene told them

what Jesus had said.

She gave them

the wonderful news

of this first Easter Day.

ABOUT THE AUTHOR

Joan Chase Bowden was born in England and spent the latter half of her school days underneath her desk during the London blitz. She began her writing career in the adult mystery magazine field, but soon found that writing for young people was more personally rewarding. This is her 14th book, her first for Concordia. Ms. Bowden has written two plays and four books for beginning readers. *A Hat for the Queen, Boo and the Flying Flews, Who Took the Top Hat Trick?* and *A New Home for Snow Ball* were nominees for the California Literature Medal Award. One of her poems, "What Happened to Alice," appears in Concordia's *Porcupine Book of Verse.* Ms. Bowden has written two books featuring Elizabeth, the youngest Walton in the television series THE WALTONS. She lives in San Diego with her husband and their three children.